The Ashenda Girl

A Celebration of Girls, Freedom, and Joy!

by Dr. Magi Tareke

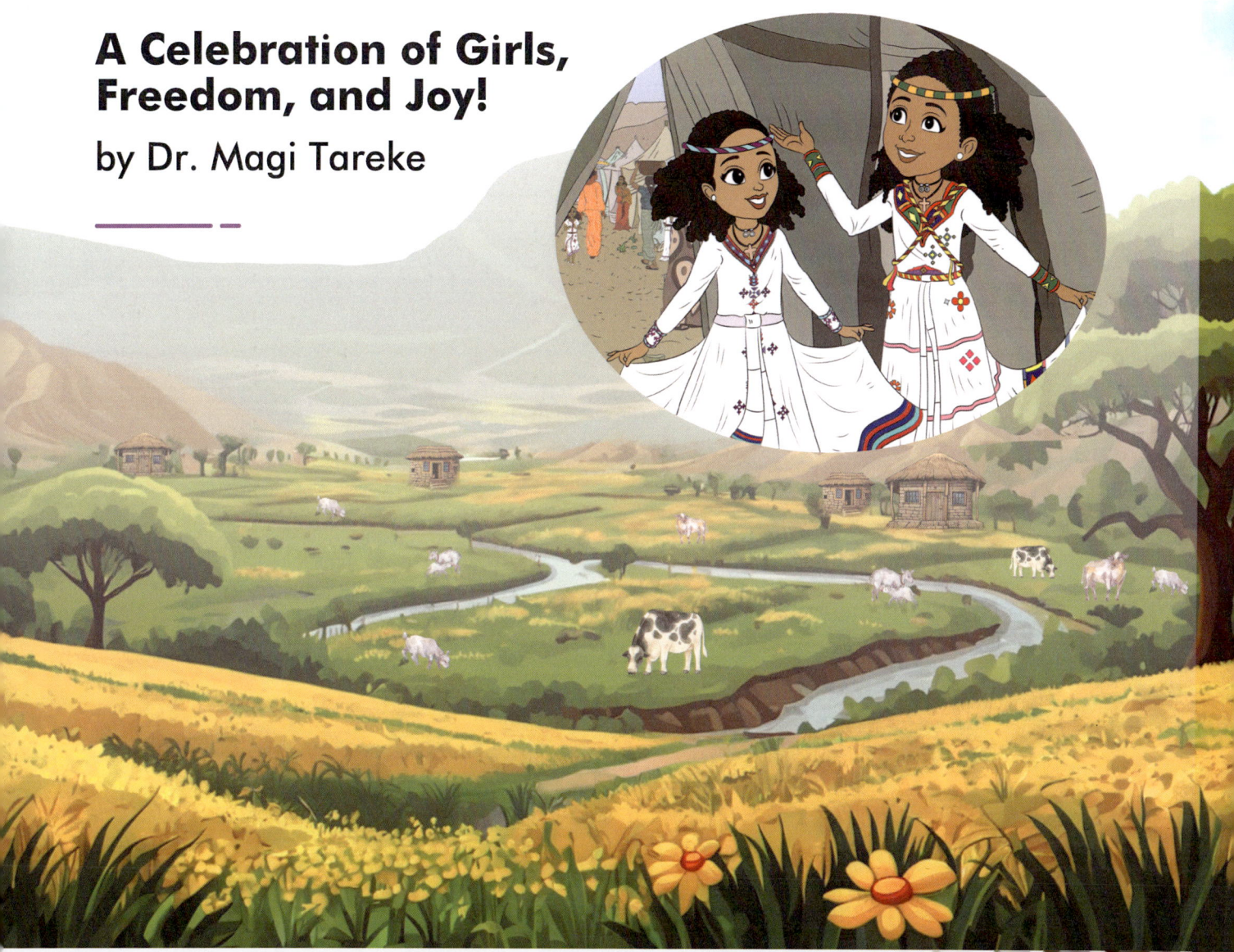

Published by Hasmark Publishing International
www.hasmarkpublishing.com

Copyright © 2024 Magi Tareke
First Edition

No part of this book may be reproduced or transmitted in any form or by any means, electronic or mechanical, including photocopying, recording, or by any information storage and retrieval system, without written permission from the author, except for the inclusion of brief quotations in a review.

Disclaimer:
This book is designed to provide information and motivation to our readers. It is sold with the understanding that the publisher is not engaged to render any type of psychological, legal, or any other kind of professional advice. The content of each article is the sole expression and opinion of its author, and not necessarily that of the publisher. No warranties or guarantees are expressed or implied by the publisher's choice to include any of the content in this volume. Neither the publisher nor the individual author(s) shall be liable for any physical, psychological, emotional, financial, or commercial damages, including, but not limited to, special, incidental, consequential or other damages. Our views and rights are the same: You are responsible for your own choices, actions, and results.

Permission should be addressed in writing to Mearg Tareke at Hello@magitareke.com
Author Name: Dr. Mearg (Magi) Tareke
Illustrator: scribbleline
Cover Design: Anne Karklins (anne@hasmarkpublishing.com)
Interior Layout: Scott Harrer (scott@scottharrer.com)

ISBN 13: 978-1-77482-300-2
ISBN 10: 1-77482-300-4

Proceeds from all book sales will be donated to **My Shoes Your Shoes** nonprofit organization to advance their mission of helping girls in refugee camps by providing shoes and school supplies.

Rigat woke up with her heart racing in excitement on a bright August morning.

The camp around her buzzed with life as sounds of laughter and music filled the air. Together with her older sister, Lidya, Rigat was about to discover the magic of Ashenda,
a Tigrayan celebration that celebrates freedom and culture.

OH, IT'S ASHENDA DAY

DEDICATION

To all the girls in the Tunaydbah refugee camp in Sudan, especially to sisters Rigat and Lidya, whose strength and love for life have inspired me to write this story. You have taught me that hope and joy can be found even in the darkest of times. This book is dedicated to your wild spirits.

Magi

ACKNOWLEDGMENTS

I want to express my gratitude to you, GOD, for putting these girls on my path, for allowing me to help them, and for sharing a part of my life with them. Thank you, Lord Jesus Christ!

To all the girls in the refugee camp for inspiring me every day.

To Daniel Gebreamlak, Dr. Tegest Hailu, and all the members of the My Shoes Your Shoes organization: your efforts and dedication have made a significant difference in countless lives.

To all the mentors and colleagues who have accompanied me during this journey, none of this would have been possible without your guidance and encouragement. Thank you for believing in me and helping me bring my vision to life.

THIS BOOK BELONGS TO

_____

Rigat woke up with a start, her heart racing with excitement. A bright August morning ray of sunshine slipped through the tent's window, waking her up. Her older sister, Lidya, was still asleep, while outside, the camp was already buzzing with people. The laughter of children echoed in the distance, and Rigat wondered if today was the special day.

With her heart pounding, Rigat peeked outside.

Two girls in beautiful dresses with flowers in their hair passed by, humming a song. Farther away, a little girl, also very elegant, was stepping out of her tent. Her parents kissed her goodbye and watched as she left.

Rigat hurried back to Lidya. She gently shook her and whispered, **"Sister, wake up."**

Lidya slowly opened her eyes and smiled at Rigat's eager expression. **"What are you doing up so early?"** she asked, stretching.

"Today's the day, isn't it?" asked Rigat, her big eyes sparkling with excitement. Lidya hugged her tight.

"Yes, Rigat, today is the big day; today is Ashenda!"

As Lidya got ready, Rigat kept asking questions: Could she learn one of those songs? Could she get a dress like the girls'? Why did the camp smell like stew? Would there be tsebhi derhō for lunch?

"Why don't we take a walk so I can explain everything to you?" Lidya suggested.

Rigat nodded eagerly, quickly putting on her sandals. Lidya took her hand, and they stepped outside.

Rigat was six years old, and Lidya was eleven. They had been living in the camp for two years; their brother, Tesfalem, had helped them get there when war broke out in their country. Although they never lacked food and the people treated them well, Rigat felt the camp was nothing like their home in Tigray. There were no mud houses, no corrals, no acacia trees—just tents and a big desert all around.

But today, everything looked different. The tents and paths were decorated with flowers and colorful fabrics—yellow and red. Flags of their region flew high, and leaves adorned every entrance. It was magical!

As the sisters strolled around the camp, they came across a group of girls chatting and laughing. They wore white dresses with colorful embroidery. Beaded necklaces, coins, and silver crosses hung from their necks. Some girls braided their hair in fancy designs, while others hung long green leaves around their waists.

"I love their dresses!" Rigat said.

"They are called Tilfi," Lidya replied. "And the hairstyle also has a name. It's called Kunano."

"Kunano," Rigat repeated to herself. She walked a few steps thoughtfully, and then said, "If I had a Tilfi, I would wear it every day!"

Lidya smiled. "We wear them only on very special occasions."

"Like Ashenda!" Rigat exclaimed.

"Exactly," Lidya said. "Ashenda began as a celebration to honor our mother, the Virgin Mary. It takes place after the two weeks of Filseta fasting. On the morning of Ashenda, the first thing we do is go to the church for a blessing before the singing and dancing start. Nowadays, it's a celebration for all women, and people of all religions participate."

Rigat listened to her sister as she looked around, fascinated. Lidya knelt down and looked her in the eyes. "Today is our day, Rigat," she explained proudly. "Today, we celebrate being girls, and we don't need to worry about anything else—we're free!"

Rigat's eyes sparkled with curiosity. "Free? What do you mean? Like, we have nothing to do today?"

Her voice was filled with wonder, as if the concept of freedom was a magical gift she had just discovered.

"Yes, it means we have all day for us," Lidya said with a smile.

"Back home, women and girls are expected to do housework every day. Well, during Ashenda, no one will ask us to do any of that. Today we put on our prettiest clothes, receive blessings in church, and dance all day."

Rigat could hardly believe it!
a whole day just to have fun
and celebrate?
It sounded too good
to be true!

As they strolled through the camp, they saw a group of girls singing and dancing to the drums. Their voices filled the air with joyful melodies. "**Ashenda, Ashenda!**" they chanted, creating beautiful harmony.

Nearby, some boys stood holding sticks like brave warriors. Rigat tugged at her sister's dress. **"Are those boys also part of Ashenda?"** Lidya thought for a moment.

"They are, but in a different way. The boys help ensure we can sing and dance safely; they protect us on our special day."

As Rigat watched the celebrations around her, a mix of excitement and nervousness grew inside her. She turned to her sister and asked shyly, **"Lidya…can I celebrate too?"** Lidya laughed and clapped her hands, amused.

"Of course you can celebrate, Rigat! That's the idea. Come, let's get you dressed." She took Rigat's hand and led her back to the tent.

Together, they rummaged through their small trunk of clothes. Lidya pulled out a dress that Rigat had never seen before.

"This was mine when I was your age," Lidya said softly. **"Now it's yours."**

The dress was a beautiful shade of purple with red patterns. Rigat put it on, spinning to watch the skirt flare. Then Lidya sat her down and braided her hair in Kunano style.

When the hair was done, she pulled out some jewels from a small box and handed them to Rigat one by one. **"This is called Weleba; it goes in your hair,"** Lidya said as she carefully placed it in Rigat's hair.

Rigat touched the Weleba gently. **"It's so beautiful!"** she whispered.

Lidya then took out another item from the box. **"And this one is a Gobagub. It goes around your neck,"** she added, draping the necklace around Rigat's neck.

Rigat smiled as she admired the Gobagub, feeling proud to wear something so special.

As a final touch, Lidya tied a colorful band around Rigat's waist. "There," she said, stepping back. "You look beautiful. Now you're really ready for Ashenda."

Lidya wore a white Tilfi dress with colorful embroidery. She had a red and yellow band around her waist, adorned with green leaves.

Well dressed and groomed, Lidya and Rigat made their way to the camp church, where a small crowd had gathered. One by one, the girls passed in front of the priest, who gave them a cross to kiss and blessed them. When Rigat's turn came, the priest, with his hand on her forehead, said a prayer for her. She felt important; today was her day too

After the blessing, a group of girls spotted her. **"Rigat!"** one of them shouted, signaling her to come closer. Rigat looked at Lidya, who gave her an encouraging nod. With a deep breath, Rigat let go of her sister's hand and ran to join the girls.

Together, they formed a joyful procession through the camp. They sang songs about friendship and joy, and Rigat, who had been shy at first, was soon caught up in the excitement.

As they danced, Rigat noticed how everyone in the camp seemed to stop and smile at them. Even the elders, usually so serious, greeted them cheerfully as they passed by.

Between songs and dances, the girls shared freshly baked bread lovingly prepared by the women of the camp. And even though nobody had much money around there, many people still came forward to give them coins!

As the sun began to set, painting the sky in brilliant shades of orange and pink, Rigat ran back to her sister Lidya. She had wrapped the tall, green grass called "**Ashenda**" around her waist and was laughing as she played with her friends. When she saw Lidya, Rigat gave her a big hug. Her heart felt warm and full.

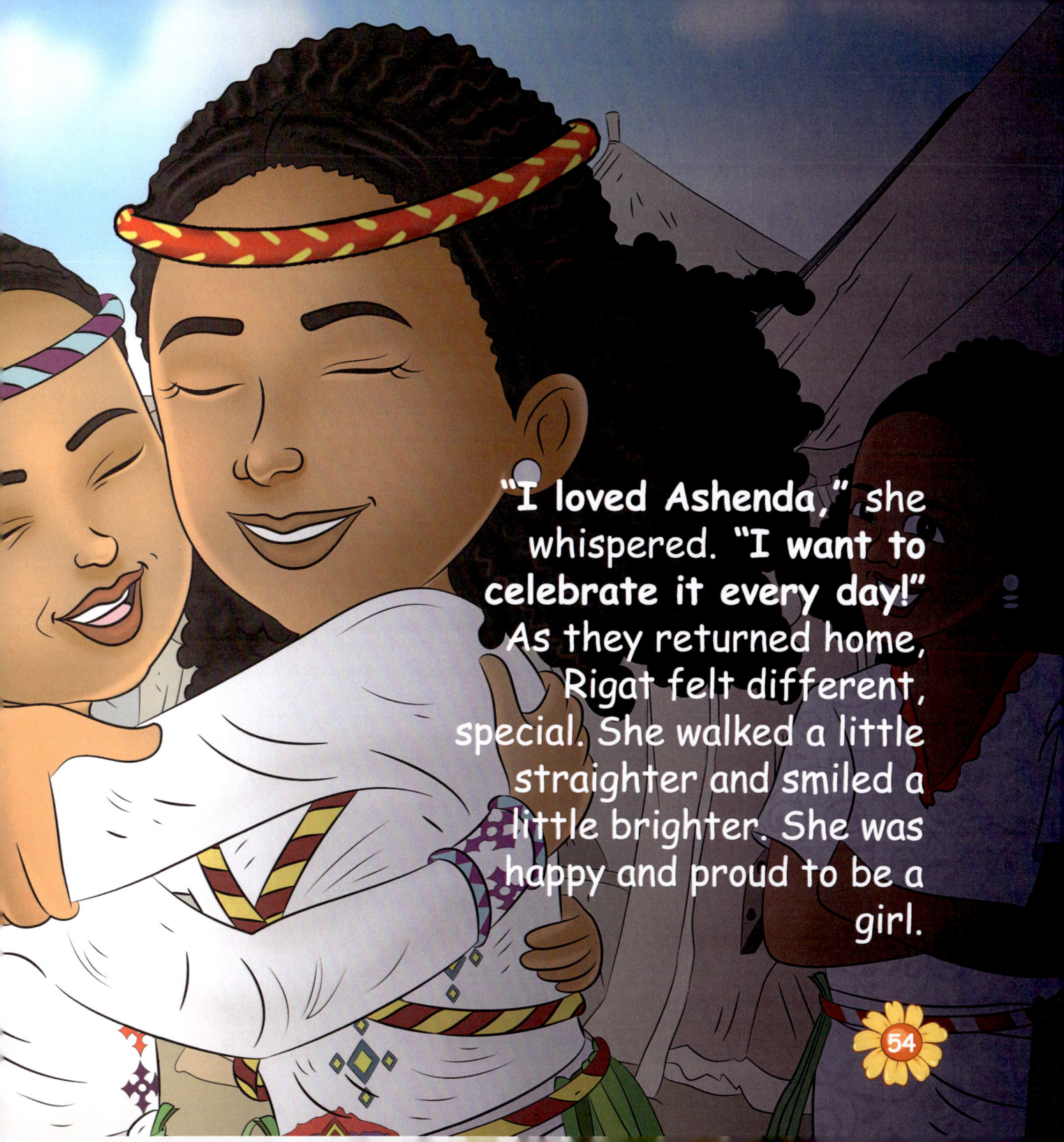

That night, as Lidya slept peacefully, Rigat lay on her back next to her, remembering the songs and all the beautiful things she had seen that day. Being a girl was something special, and being free felt good and important. She touched the beads in her hair and smiled, recalling the dances and the blessing from the priest. Today had felt like coming home.

As she drifted off to sleep, Rigat found herself surrounded by her family: Lidya, Tesfalem, Mom, and Dad were all there, singing and dancing. Even though they were far away, Ashenda had brought them to her; it was true that she had been blessed.

Dr. Magi Tareke during her Visit Sudan Refugee camp 2022 with Rigat.

About The Author

Dr. Mearg Tareke, also known as Magi, is a native of Adwa in the Tigray region of Ethiopia. Growing up in a humble community, Magi was deeply moved by the image of young girls arriving at school barefoot, their feet bruised and battered. That sight sparked something within her. That is why Magi promised herself that, when she had the opportunity, she would help give shoes to girls in need.

Magi completed high school in Adwa and graduated in pharmacy in Gondar, Ethiopia. She worked for a year in Addis Ababa and then, in 2011, managed to move to the United States. There, Magi started a new life, but she never forgot her promise. She pursued her education with determination and went on to earn her Doctorate in Pharmacy from Shenandoah University in Virginia in 2019. She then created My Shoes Your Shoes, a nonprofit organization that provides shoes and school supplies to girls in developing countries.

In 2021, civil war broke out in Tigray, causing great suffering and mass emigration. In 2022, Magi traveled to Tunaydbah refugee camp in Sudan to distribute shoes, school supplies, and medicine. She also helped organize the celebration of Ashenda, a day on which women and girls celebrate their femininity and honor their culture. It was the beauty and resilience Magi saw in those girls that inspired her to write this book.

Magi is an activist, humanitarian, and fashion enthusiast. Today, she is dedicated to helping women and children through education and empowerment. She believes that strengthening the family is the most effective way to improve the community and is convinced of the impact she can make by helping one girl at a time.

www.ingramcontent.com/pod-product-compliance
Lightning Source LLC
Chambersburg PA
CBRC091452160426
43209CB00023B/1877